To Mary Trask — AL

For Craig, my never-flagging companion on the journey upstream — KR

Salmon Creek

Annette LeBox

PICTURES BY

Karen Reczuch

Groundwood Books

House of Anansi Press

Toronto Berkeley

THESE were Sumi's first memories:
water over stones,
the scent of creek,
darkness so complete
she could barely imagine
another world larger
than the egg case enclosing her.

Sumi was blind,
but she could hear the wind
whispering through the cedars.
She could hear the creek stones
lifting and falling as the salmon mothers built
     their nests.
And if she pressed against the curve of her egg,
she could hear her salmon mother singing.

Home is the scent of cedar and creek.
Home is the journey's end.

At dusk, a bear wandered down to the creek.
He sat on his haunches, feasting on salmon.
Beneath the creek, Sumi turned in her egg,
strained to hear from her little stone bed,
a song of a journey, a seed of a dream.

I followed the stars and the river's pull.
I followed the salty air.
The sea was wide and beautiful,
but my heart wasn't there.

And later, as the salmon mothers drifted gently downstream,
their songs grew fainter…

A windstorm shook the last of the maple leaves from the trees.

The leaves fell on the mossy log, then joined the creek.

A flock of eagles picked at the salmon bones left by the bear.

The scent of salmon lingered in the air.

Sumi slept until mid-winter.

When she woke, she could see.

She had two large eyes and a delicate tail.

She carried a yolk sac beneath her.

Thrusting her tail against her sac,

she pushed and pushed

till her egg case split open,

and she tumbled head first into the creek.

She was as small as a pine needle,
scared and alone.
She hid beneath the gravel
till her strength had grown.
When her egg sac was empty,
she swam upward,
followed a school of fry.

She widened her nostrils,
memorized each scent:
moss and fern and cedar,
maple and damp earth!
Her birth creek. Home.

As the days became warmer,
Algae grew on Salmon Creek.
Ducks dabbled in the bright green bloom.
Dragonflies and mayflies fed there,
and the fry fed on insects and larvae.

Sumi swam in quiet pools,
hunted among schools of silver fry,
hid from the heron's watchful eye.

Summer turned to fall.

When winter came, snow fell on Salmon Creek.

A raccoon crept silently through the icy stream.

Beneath a root, Sumi woke and slept,

dreaming of spring.

Spring arrived again with a torrent of water.
Rushing, rumbling, roaring, tumbling!
The current carried the fry, head first, downstream,
past ducks and herons with hungry beaks,
past gulls and dippers eager to feast.
The creek hurled the fry over rocks and sweepers,
tossed them against roots and tangled creepers.

Sumi's fins grew battered and her tail torn,
but the current drove her on and on and on
till she reached the river
where the banks grew steeper,
the rapids stronger,
the water deeper.

As she swam down the river,
her side stripes faded,
Her skin secreted a fine mucous coat,
Her body grew longer and sleeker and stronger.
And one morning she woke to find herself a smolt.

She swam past factories and farms and forests.
She swam past tug boats and log booms and small towns.
She swam past docks and cottages and children playing
till she came to a place where the river meets the sea.

She circled the estuary, gazed out at the bay,
to the water beyond, where her new home lay.

Then she smelled something sweeter than her birth creek
in spring,
sweeter than the fragrance of cedar and stones,
a salt-sweet memory buried deep in her bones.
The sea!

As she tasted salt water, her body felt strange.
Little by little, her insides changed.
Then she joined a school of salt drinking smolts,
ready at last to swim to the sea.

On sunny days when the sea was filled with a pale green light,
Sumi herded herring into sea caves or lazed in beds of kelp.

She learned to dodge the nets of fishermen and dive from whales and seals.
She feasted on sand lance and candlefish
and shrimp-like creatures called krill!
The krill turned her flesh a brilliant pink.

As the months passed, her body grew longer,
her scales brighter, her muscles stronger.

And then, one summer everything changed.
Perhaps it was the eggs forming deep inside her,
that made Sumi yearn for the creek of her birth,
that made her remember the scent of damp earth,
or an algae bloom on a summer night,
or the taste of a mayfly caught midflight.

Then Sumi set out for the stream of her birth.
She followed the stars and the pull of the earth.
Heart racing, she traced her journey homeward,
back to the place where the river meets the sea.

The estuary was crowded, she was not alone!
Thousands of salmon were heading home.

They entered the river, spell-bound, scales glistening,
life quickening within them, river streaming over their gills,
bellies swelling with eggs and milt, no longer eating,
no longer sleeping, fighting the river's will.

Sumi climbed up rapids, and leaped over falls.
She dove under logs and roaring torrents.
She rode the currents, her muscles straining,
her fins tattered, her strength waning,
but she wouldn't stop, she couldn't stop...

till she came to a creek with a wonderful smell.
And she swam up that creek as if caught in a spell.

A silvery gang of salmon raced by her.
And among them, Nulluk, searching for a mate.
He swam towards Sumi, nuzzling her sides.

Sumi leaped from the creek, fins outspread,
arched her back and shot ahead.
Nulluk followed her leap,
shadowed each fin stroke.

As Sumi swam in fresh water, her body felt strange.
The salmon around her began to change.
The males grew fangs and fierce hooked noses.
Their scales became the color of roses.
Their crowns grew green as leaves in spring.

And then one morning they swam to a place
where an ancient cedar leaned over a stream,
where the water ran a pure pale green,
where the stones shimmered with a golden sheen.

And Sumi knew by the smell and the taste
that *this* was her birth place, the place she loved best.
A perfect place to build her nest!

She lay on her side, waved her tail like a cat.
She slapped the water, till the stones parted.
And in the hollow, she laid thousands of eggs
like pale orange suns, sinking into the silt.
Then Nulluk showered her eggs with milt,
and the water of the creek flowed white, like milk.
And quickly, gently, Sumi flicked her tail,
and the gravel drifted into the nest,
covering her eggs, like secrets.

Sumi and Nulluk drifted in the shallows.
They were spawned out, exhausted.
Their sides were battered, their fins torn.
Their skin had thickened, their scales worn.
But they had chased a dream and caught it.
They had swum all the way to the sea and back.

Sumi circled the creek, guarding her eggs.
She bared her curved teeth, slapped her tail,
scared off pairs of spawners from her redd.

Sumi gazed at the sky.

It was radiant, a deep blue green.

She could hear the wind

whispering through the cedars.

She could hear the creek stones lifting and falling

as the salmon mothers built their nests.

Small insects nestled in the folds of her skin.

And later, as she drifted gently downstream,

Sumi sang to her eggs…

Home is the scent of cedar and creek.

Home is the journey's end.

At dusk, a bear wandered down to the creek.
It sat on its haunches, feasting on salmon.

A windstorm shook the last of the maple leaves from the trees.
The leaves fell on the mossy log, then joined the creek.
A flock of eagles picked at the salmon bones left by the bear.
The scent of salmon lingered in the air.

The Life Cycle of the Coho Salmon

THERE ARE FIVE different species of salmon that begin their lives in the waters of the Pacific Northwest — sockeye, chinook, pink, chum and coho. Each species has a unique appearance as well as different spawning habits and life cycles. This timeline shows the life cycle of the coho salmon.

1. In the late fall, usually November, the female coho lays eggs in the gravel of her freshwater birth creek. The male coho fertilizes the eggs with a white substance called milt. Eleven or twelve days later, the male and female salmon die.

2. In December or January, the eggs hatch. The tiny salmon, called alevins, remain in the gravel, living on food from their yolk sacs.

3. By March or April, the young salmon lose their yolk sacs. They are now known as fry. The fry swim into the open water of the creek to hunt for food. They have dark stripes on their sides called parr marks which help to camouflage them from predators.

4. In late April or May after spending a year in the creek, the young, now called smolts, begin to migrate down the river. The dark parr marks slowly fade and a silver coating develops on their scales. This process of adapting to sea water is called smoltification.

November | December | January | February | March | April | May | June | July | August | September | October | November | December | January | February | March

5. The smolts' journey to the estuary, where the river meets the sea, may take days, weeks or even months depending on how far away their birth creek is. There is plenty of food in the estuary, and as they pass through, the smolts eat as much as they can, growing larger and stronger before swimming to the sea. By late June, when the smolts enter the sea, they have developed dark blue-black backs with silvery sides and bellies. Most of their parr marks have disappeared. The smolts' new appearance allows them to blend in with the ocean environment.

6. The young coho spend sixteen to eighteen months in the sea, eating and growing. Early the next summer, the fully grown coho begin their homeward migration. It may take them up to six months to reach fresh water.

7. As the coho enter fresh water, they stop eating and live on the fat stored in their bodies. Their skin becomes thick and leathery. The male coho develops a hooked snout. The female's body swells with ripening eggs.

8. By the time the coho reach their birth creek in November, they have developed dark red sides and dark green backs and heads. The female coho lays her eggs in the gravel of the creek and the cycle begins again.

June   July   August   September   October   November   December   January   February   March   April   May   June   July   August   September   October   November

Threats to Pacific Salmon

PACIFIC SALMON are in danger because they are losing their natural habitats and because too many of them are being caught.

Climate changes in our world, including global warming, affect the waters where the salmon live. As rivers become warmer, and their water levels lower, fewer salmon are able to swim all the way back to their spawning grounds.

Often the salmon's habitats are damaged by pollution. Wastes from sewage disposal systems, factories and sawmills contain substances that are harmful to fish. Even in our own gardens and homes, insecticides, fertilizers and household detergents are sometimes poured down drains into the water system. These pollutants end up in rivers and oceans.

Careless logging practices destroy many salmon streams. When logs are driven down shallow rivers, they can block them. Clear-cutting a forest can make soil or silt run into nearby streams and rivers. This destroys the salmon's eggs and clogs their gills so that they are unable to breathe.

When we construct new buildings, parking lots and roads, the land is stripped of the trees and plants that hold the soil in place. Rain pours down bare hillsides into streams, causing erosion, a build-up of silt and flooding, all of which can kill spawning salmon.

One of the biggest threats to salmon are hydroelectric dams. Many fish die in their attempt to leap over a dam as they return to their spawning grounds. And even if they are successful, they often find themselves in an artificial lake instead of their familiar birth stream.

Finally, too many salmon are being caught because there are not enough controls over where and when people fish. Some people think the solution is to "farm" salmon in pens made of nets placed in the ocean.

But many scientists think that this practice is harmful to wild salmon. The farmed fish may spread diseases to the wild fish. And if farmed fish escape and mate with wild salmon, then the wild fish will eventually become weaker.

If we do not change our fishing practices and protect the salmon's natural habitat, this magnificent fish may be lost to us forever.

How Kids Can Help

• Join the Pacific Streamkeepers Federation (www.pskf.ca), an organization that provides practical guidance for stream and wetland care for volunteers of all ages who want to help protect local waterways in British Columbia. The federation is supported by the Department of Fisheries and Oceans Salmonid Enhancement Program in Vancouver, B.C. It is modeled after stream stewardship programs in the United States such as the Adopt-A-Stream Foundation in Everett, Washington. Visit www.streamkeeper.org.

• Pick up any garbage that you see in a creek or stream.

• Ask an adult to help you write to government officials to tell them that you are concerned about wild salmon.

Glossary

Alevin A newly hatched salmon that still has its yolk sac attached.

Estuary The mouth of a river where fresh water mixes with salt water.

Fertilize The process in which an egg and a sperm join to produce a baby salmon.

Fry The name for the stage at which the young salmon have used up their egg sacs and are ready to find their own food.

Migrate To travel from one place to another when the seasons change.

Milt A milky fluid that contains the male's sperm, which fertilizes the female's eggs.

Redd The area of a spawning stream where a female salmon chooses to dig several nests.

Scales The thin, flat overlapping plates made of a soft bonelike material that cover the body of a salmon.

Smolt The stage when the young salmon begins its migration toward the sea. The process is gradual and continues until the juvenile salmon loses its stripes and turns silver which indicates its readiness to adapt to salt water.

Spawn To produce eggs or sperm; also a term used to describe the fertilization of the eggs.

Species A type or kind of plant or animal.

Sperm A substance produced by the male salmon to fertilize the female's eggs.

Yolk sac The large orange sac attached to the baby salmon that holds all the food the salmon needs until it is big enough to find food for itself.

For Further Reading and Viewing

For young readers:

Come Back, Salmon by Molly Cone. How a group of dedicated kids adopted Pigeon Creek in Everett, Washington, and brought it back to life. Contains color photographs. (Sierra Club Books for Children, 1992)

The Salmon (Life Cycles) by Sabrina Crewe, illustrated by Colin Newman. Describes the habitat, eating habits and life cycle of the sockeye salmon in photographs and illustrations. (Raintree/Steck-Vaughn Publishers, 1998)

Salmon Stream (A Sharing Nature With Children Book) by Carol Reed-Jones, illustrated by Michael S. Maydak. Words and colorful pictures capture the Pacific salmon's mysterious life cycle. (Dawn Publications, 2001)

For older readers:

Salmon Nation: People and Fish at the Edge edited by Edward C. Wolf and Seth Zuckerman. A fascinating book published by the EcoTrust Foundation, a non-profit organization dedicated to building a conservation economy in the coastal temperate rain forest region of North America. (Distributed by Greystone Books, 2002)

Video

A Last Wild Salmon, video from Filmwest Associates, 2399 Hayman Road, Kelowna, B.C. V1Z 1Z8. Toll free fax: 1-800-570-5505; email: info@filmwest.com or visit www.filmwest.com. The odyssey of a Pacific salmon. An inspiring hour-long film with haunting music and spectacular shots.

ACKNOWLEDGMENTS

I would like to acknowledge Ross Davies and Janice Jarvis for their assistance. I am especially grateful to Bruce Clark of the Department of Fisheries and Oceans for his valuable suggestions and his patience in answering my endless questions.

AL

Groundwood Books / House of Anansi Press
110 Spadina Avenue, Suite 801, Toronto, Ontario, M5V 2K4

Distributed in the USA by Publishers Group West
1700 Fourth Street, Berkeley, CA 94710

We acknowledge for their financial support of our publishing program the Canada Council for the Arts, the Government of Canada through the Book Publishing Industry Development Program (BPIDP), the Ontario Arts Council and the Government of Ontario through the Ontario Media Development Corporation's Ontario Book Initiative.

ONTARIO ARTS COUNCIL
CONSEIL DES ARTS DE L'ONTARIO

Library and Archives Canada Cataloguing in Publication
LeBox, Annette
Salmon Creek
ISBN-13 978-0-88899-458-5 (bound).– ISBN-13 978-0-88899-644-2 (pbk.)
ISBN-10 0-88899-458-3 (bound).– ISBN-10 0-88899-644-6 (pbk.)
Salmon—Juvenile fiction. I. Reczuch, Karen. II. Title.
PS8573.E3364S34 2001   jC813'.54   C2001-901568-2
PR9199.3.L368S34 2001

Library of Congress Control Number: 2002102162

Book design by Michael Solomon
The illustrations are done in watercolor.
Printed and bound in China by Everbest Printing Co. Ltd.